A+ books

NATURE RIDDLES

# MYSTERY ANIMAL TRACKS

## A Photo Riddle Book

By Kelly Barnhill

CAPSTONE PRESS
a capstone imprint

A+ Books are published by Capstone Press,
151 Good Counsel Drive, P.O. Box 669, Mankato, Minnesota 56002.
www.capstonepress.com

092009
005620LKS10

 Books published by Capstone Press are manufactured with paper
containing at least 10 percent post-consumer waste.

*Library of Congress Cataloging-in-Publication Data*

Barnhill, Kelly Regan.
    Mystery animal tracks : a photo riddle book / by Kelly Barnhill.
    p. cm. — (A+ books. nature riddles)
    Includes bibliographical references and index.
    Summary: "Photographs and simple text present a variety of animal tracks and facts
about the animals that make them" — Provided by publisher.
    ISBN 978-1-4296-3921-7 (library binding)
    1. Animal tracks — Juvenile literature. I. Title. II. Series.
QL768.B38 2010
591.47'9 — dc22
                                                2009040498

**Credits**

Jenny Marks, editor; Veronica Bianchini, designer; Svetlana Zhurkin, media researcher;
    Laura Manthe, production specialist

**Photo Credits**

Alamy/blickwinkel, 8
Dreamstime/Damien Richard, 23
Getty Images/The Image Bank/Joseph Van Os, 20; Jeffrey Phelps, 17; National Geographic/Jim
    and Jamie Dutcher, 11; Visuals Unlimited/Barbara Hesse, 19
iStockphoto/Aldo Murillo, 29; Andrej Štojs, 14; Robert Koopmans, 15
Minden Pictures/Mark Raycroft, 25, 26; Pete Oxford, 22
Shutterstock/Andreas68, 21; B.G. Smith, 18; Dmitry Pichugin, 13; Eduard Kyslynskyy, 16; Eric
    Isselée, cover; Jarrod Erbe, 9; Melinda Fawver, 4–5; Michael Ledray, 27; Oksana Petrova, 24;
    Petr Mašek, 12; wrangler, 10; zimmytws, 6–7
Steve Weston, 28
Ted Barnhill, 32

**Note to Parents, Teachers, and Librarians**

Nature Riddles uses a nonfiction riddle format to introduce science concepts to young readers.
*Mystery Animal Tracks* is designed to be read aloud to a pre-reader, or to be read independently
by an early reader. Deciphering word riddles and analyzing photos engages readers' critical
thinking skills and heightens visual literacy. Nature Riddles promotes practice of the scientific
inquiry process, through engaging children in observing, analyzing, guessing, and solving each
science riddle.

# TABLE OF CONTENTS

# INTRODUCTION

In nature, we are not alone. Field mice scurry under dry leaves. Squirrels race down bumpy tree trunks. Sleepy bears creep out of their caves and yawn.

But if we can't see them, how do we know which animals are nearby? And how do we find them? To find the hidden animals, we have to find their tracks first.

A track is the shape of an animal's foot, paw, or hoof that has been pressed into the ground.

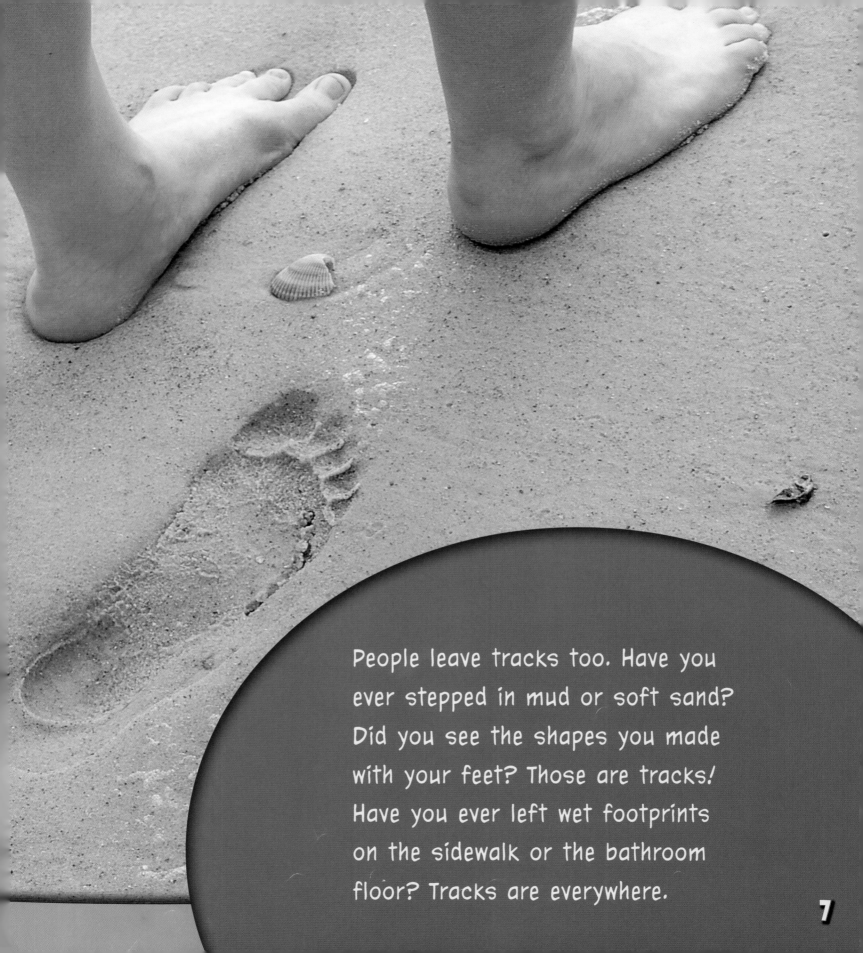

People leave tracks too. Have you ever stepped in mud or soft sand? Did you see the shapes you made with your feet? Those are tracks! Have you ever left wet footprints on the sidewalk or the bathroom floor? Tracks are everywhere.

Tracks are clues to who's been walking nearby. Small, dainty animals leave tiny, faint tracks. Heavy animals make deep tracks. Each kind of animal leaves its own special mark.

CAN YOU GUESS ...

... WHICH ANIMALS LEFT THE TRACKS IN EACH PICTURE?

8

# HANDPRINT BANDIT

See my tiny handprints
in the dirt beside the shed?
See the little footprints made
when I stole some bread?
I have 10 fingers and 10 toes,
but human I am not.
My black-ringed tail and robber's mask
make me easier to spot.

## WHO AM I?

# A RACCOON!

Raccoons are very clever. They use their fingers to open garbage cans and to dig for grubs. They even peel the husks off ears of corn!

# HUNGRY HOWLER

If you follow in my tracks,
you'll find me hunting
with my pack.
We travel fast
past streams and hills.
We catch our prey
and eat our fill.
Hooowwwl!

## WHO AM I ?

# A WOLF!

A wolf's tracks look similar to dog tracks. But when dogs run, they sway from side to side. Wolves run in a straight line. Their tracks are easy to follow.

# SLEEPING GIANT

I yawn, I stretch, I scratch my head.
I climb so slowly out of bed.
My paws sink deep into the grass.
I mark each tender blade I pass.
You will not see me in the snow
for then I'm fast asleep, you know.
But in the springtime you may see
the wide, deep tracks left by me!

## WHO AM I?

# A BEAR!

A bear's front and back paw prints are different shapes. The front tracks show an oval with toes and claws. The back tracks are about 7 inches (18 centimeters) longer!

# TINY TRAVELER

My tracks are light, thin, and small,
hardly noticeable at all.
I scurry and hide. I'm very shy,
but my paw prints show
that I've been by.

## WHO AM I?

# A MOUSE!

In summer, field mice sneak into gardens to nibble fruits and vegetables. In winter, their tiny tracks in the snow look like they're traveling on skis!

16

# SWIFT MYSTERY

My legs are long,
my hooves are small.
My tracks look like two curves
that match.
I'm thin and brown and very tall.
I'm built for speed
and tough to catch.

## WHO AM I?

# A DEER!

Although deer hooves are small, an adult deer can weigh 300 pounds (136 kilograms). Each step leaves a deep impression in the ground.

# SNEAKY STALKER

On shadowed trails I sneak and prowl.
A creature comes near, a tasty snack.
I press my wide paws to the ground.
I pounce! I grab! I drag it back.

## WHO AM I?

# A COUGAR!

Did you see any claw marks on the cougar's tracks? Cougars walk silently on their big, padded paws. They only use their claws when scratching or attacking.

# BACKWARD BOUNDER

I peek my nose out of the snow
to see if you're around.
I perk my ears and wiggle my nose.
Across the woods, I bound.
I land upon my front paws first
before my feet touch down.
That's why my back tracks are in front,
not the other way around.

## WHO AM I?

# A RABBIT!

A running rabbit leaps forward and lands on its front paws. Then he plants his hind legs in front to push off again. His tracks look like he's running backward!

## WET WADDLER

My tracks show three long toes and claws
with flaps of skin connecting each.
I waddle on land, but when I swim
I'm quick, I'm sleek, I'm out of reach.

## WHO AM I?

# A DUCK!

A duck's webbed feet are shaped like oars, and they move through water just as well. That's why ducks are such great swimmers.

# SLOW SNAPPER

See the scratches in the sand,
the track left by my heavy tail?
I don't move fast, but I don't mind.
My travels leave a patterned trail.
On each foot, I have five claws
to catch a fish or scratch and fight.
I don't have teeth, but with my beak
I grasp! I *snap!* I hold on tight!

## WHO AM I?

# A SNAPPING TURTLE!

Snapping turtles leave wavy trails along riverbanks. Their strong legs pull them slowly on land, but they swim quickly through the water.

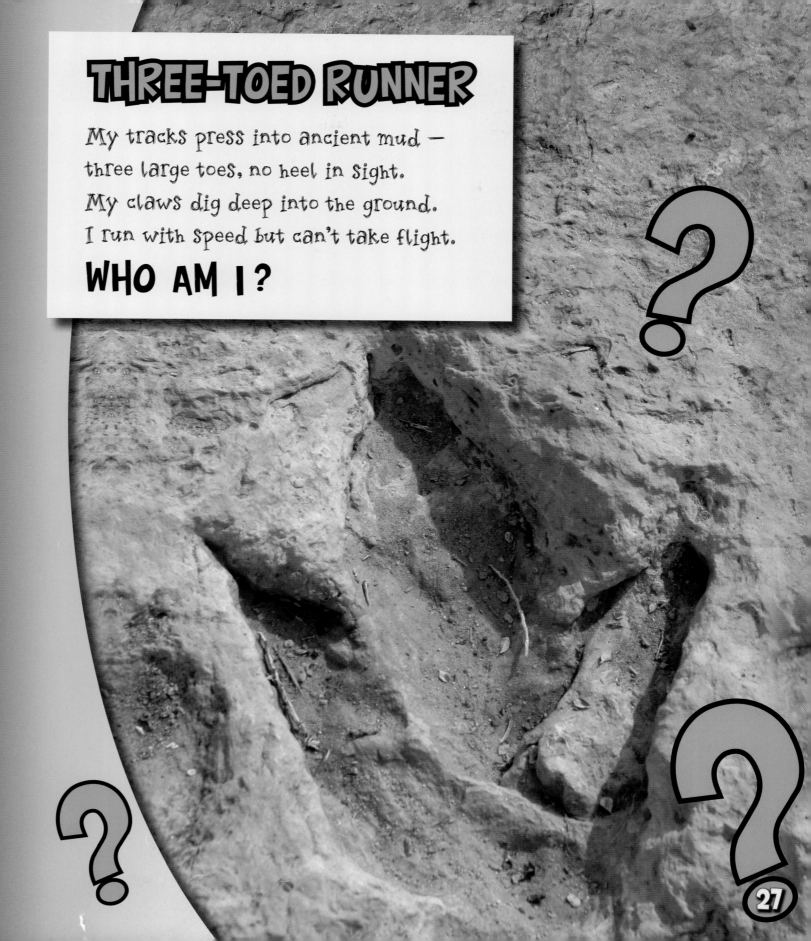

# THREE-TOED RUNNER

My tracks press into ancient mud —
three large toes, no heel in sight.
My claws dig deep into the ground.
I run with speed but can't take flight.

## WHO AM I?

# A DINOSAUR!

Millions of years ago, a hadrosaur ran across the mud. Today, you can still see that dino's mighty tracks. The mud hardened to rock, and the footprints became fossils.

Some tracks last for millions of years, but most do not. Tracks on a beach last only a moment before waves wash them away. The next time it rains, see how many tracks you can find. But don't wait too long, or they might disappear!

# GLOSSARY

**ancient** — very, very old

**clever** — able to understand and do things quickly and easily

**dainty** — small and delicate

**fossil** — the remains or traces of an animal or a plant, preserved as rock

**impression** — a shape pressed into a soft material

**oar** — a wooden pole with a wide, flat end used for rowing a boat

**pad** — the soft part at the bottom of an animal's foot

**plant** — to step down hard

**prowl** — to walk around slowly and quietly

**scurry** — to run with fast, short steps

**sleek** — smooth and shiny

# READ MORE

**Arnosky, Jim**. *Wild Tracks!: A Guide to Nature's Footprints.* New York: Sterling Publishing, 2008.

**Peterson, Megan Cooley**. *Camouflage Clues: A Photo Riddle Book.* Nature Riddles. Mankato, Minn.: Capstone Press, 2010.

**Selsam, Millicent**. *Big Tracks, Little Tracks: Following Animal Prints.* Let's-Read-and-Find-Out Science. New York: HarperCollins, 1999.

# INTERNET SITES

FactHound offers a safe, fun way to find Internet sites related to this book. All of the sites on FactHound have been researched by our staff.

Here's all you do:

Visit *www.facthound.com*

FactHound will fetch the best sites for you!

# INDEX

# ABOUT THE AUTHOR

Kelly Barnhill has always enjoyed looking things up. When she was in third grade, she said that her two favorite series of books were Nancy Drew and World Book Encyclopedia. Now that she's a grown-up, she still uses her love of mystery and discovery in her writing. She's written about animals, monsters, hoaxes, fashion, fairies, schoolteachers, sewer systems, princesses, and other subjects too numerous to name. The best part of being a writer, she thinks, is that you always get to learn something new.